U0852259

中华人民共和国文化部
2014 年文化发展统计公报

STATISTICAL COMMUNIQUÉ OF THE MINISTRY OF CULTURE OF THE PEOPLE'S REPUBLIC OF CHINA ON CULTURAL DEVELOPMENT IN 2014

中华人民共和国文化部 编

中国统计出版社
China Statistics Press

图书在版编目（CIP）数据

中华人民共和国文化部 2014 年文化发展统计公报：汉英对照 / 中华人民共和国文化部编 . -- 北京 : 中国统计出版社，2015.5

ISBN 978-7-5037-7429-4

Ⅰ . ①中… Ⅱ . ①中… Ⅲ . ①文化发展－统计分析－研究报告－中国－ 2014 －汉、英 Ⅳ . ① G12

中国版本图书馆 CIP 数据核字 (2015) 第 090675 号

中华人民共和国文化部 2014 年文化发展统计公报

作　　者 / 中华人民共和国文化部
责任编辑 / 郭　栋　李　冲
装帧设计 / 黄　晨
出版发行 / 中国统计出版社
通信地址 / 北京市西城区月坛南街 57 号
邮政编码 /100826
办公地址 / 北京市丰台区西三环南路甲 6 号
网　　址 /http://www.zgtjcbs.com
电　　话 /（010）63376877　63376907（发行部）
印　　刷 / 北京画中画印刷有限公司
经　　销 / 新华书店
开　　本 /880×1230 毫米　1/16
字　　数 /50 千字
印　　张 /2.5
版　　别 /2015 年 5 月第 1 版
版　　次 /2015 年 5 月北京第 1 次印刷
定　　价 /28.00 元

版权所有。未经许可，本书的任何部分不准以任何方式在世界任何地区以任何文字翻印、拷贝、仿制或转载。
如有印装错误，本社发行部负责调换。

目 录

CONTENTS

中华人民共和国文化部
2014 年文化发展统计公报[1]

2014 年，全国文化系统认真贯彻落实党的十八大和十八届三中、四中全会精神，深入学习领会习近平总书记系列重要讲话精神，紧紧围绕社会主义文化强国建设，培育践行社会主义核心价值观，牢固树立以人民为中心的工作导向，稳中求进，勇于担当，求真务实，积极作为，各项工作取得新突破。

一、机构和人员

年末纳入统计范围的全国文化单位[2]28.74 万个，比上年末减少 0.55 万个；从业人员[3]204.02 万人，比上年减少 11.47 万人。其中文化部门所属单位 6.56 万个，增加 872 个；从业人员 63.82 万人，与上年基本持平。

图 1　2006 年 -2014 年全国文化单位机构数及从业人员数

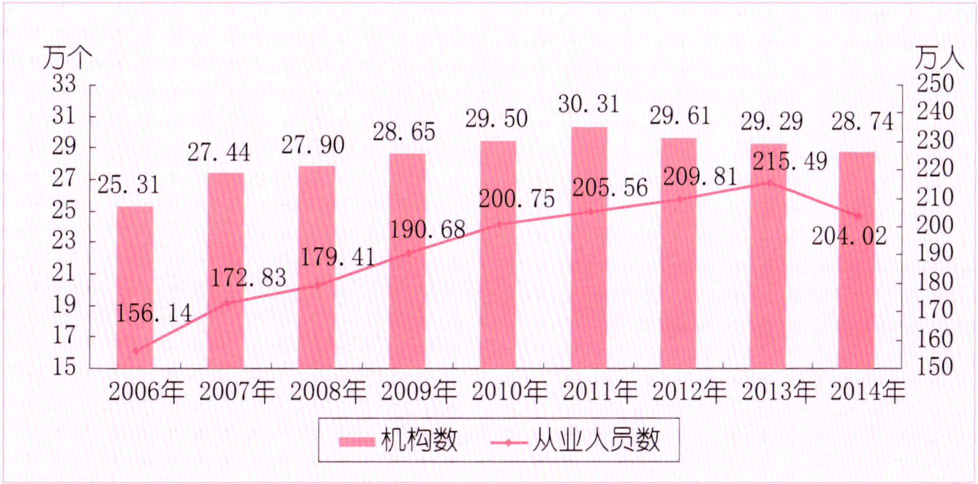

二、公共文化服务体系

2014年，文化部牵头成立国家公共文化服务体系建设协调组，形成共同会商、统筹推进的工作机制。研究起草《关于加快构建现代公共文化服务体系的意见》和《国家基本公共文化服务指导标准》，对现代公共文化服务体系进行整体制度框架设计，为全国公共文化事业的发展提供了有力保障。

（一）公共图书馆[4]

年末全国共有公共图书馆3117个，比上年末增加5个。其中少儿图书馆108个，增加3个。年末全国公共图书馆从业人员56071人，其中具有高级职称的人员5479人，占9.8%；具有中级职称的人员18146人，占32.4%。

年末全国公共图书馆实际使用房屋建筑面积1231.60万平方米，比上年末增长6.3%；图书总藏量[5]79092万册，增长5.6%；电子图书50674万册，增长34.2%；阅览室座席数85.55万个，增长5.7%；计算机19.86万台，增长1.6%；供读者使用的电子阅览终端12.16万台，增长4.6%。

年末全国平均每万人公共图书馆建筑面积90.0平方米，比上年末增加4.9平方米；全国人均图书藏量0.58册，比上年增加0.03册；全国人均购书费1.24元，比上年增加0.02元。

图2　2006年–2014年全国公共图书馆人均资源情况

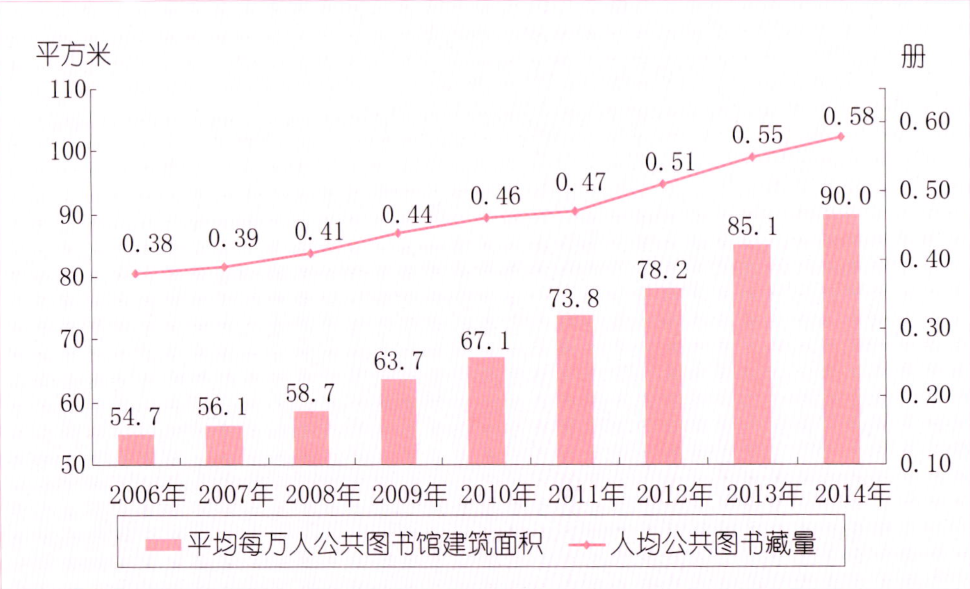

全年全国公共图书馆发放借书证[6]3944万个，比上年增长37.1%；总流通人次[7]53036万，增长7.7%。书刊文献外借册次46734万，增长14.4%；外借人次22737万，增长10.6%。全年共为读者举办各种活动103586次，增长13.2%；参加人次5015万，增长13.7%。

图 3　2006 年 -2014 年全国公共图书馆总流通人次及书刊外借册次

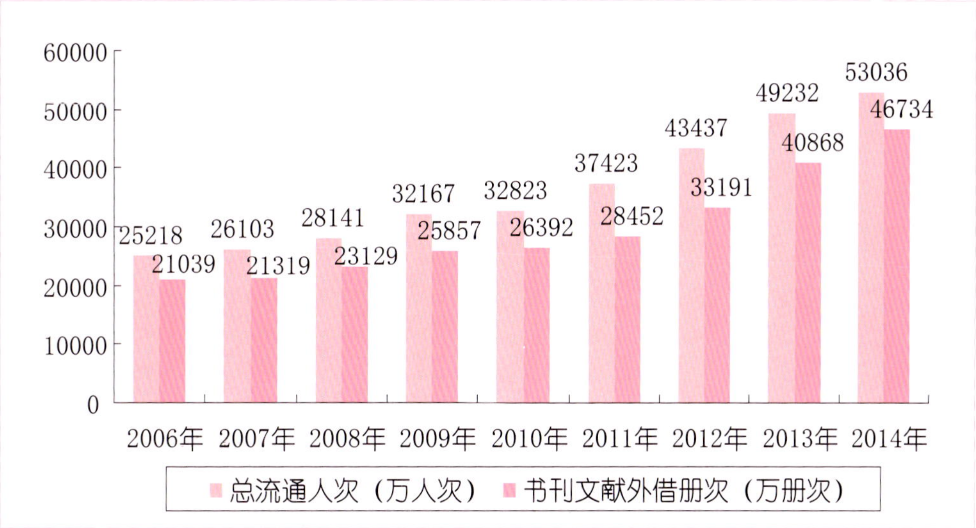

（二）群众文化机构[8]

年末全国共有群众文化机构 44423 个，比上年末增加 163 个。其中乡镇综合文化站 34465 个，增加 122 个。年末全国群众文化机构从业人员 170299 人，比上年末增加 5944 人。其中具有高级职称的人员 5633 人，占 3.3%；具有中级职称的人员 16605 人，占 9.8%。

年末全国群众文化机构实际使用房屋建筑面积 3686.39 万平方米，比上年末增长 8.8%；藏书 2.48 亿册，增长 7.8%；计算机 34.67 万台，增长 18.6%；对公众开放的阅览室 108.02 万平方米，增长 8.3%。年末全国平均每万人群众文化设施建筑面积 269.51 平方米，比上年末提高 20.42 平方米。

图 4　2006 年 -2014 年全国平均每万人群众文化设施建筑面积

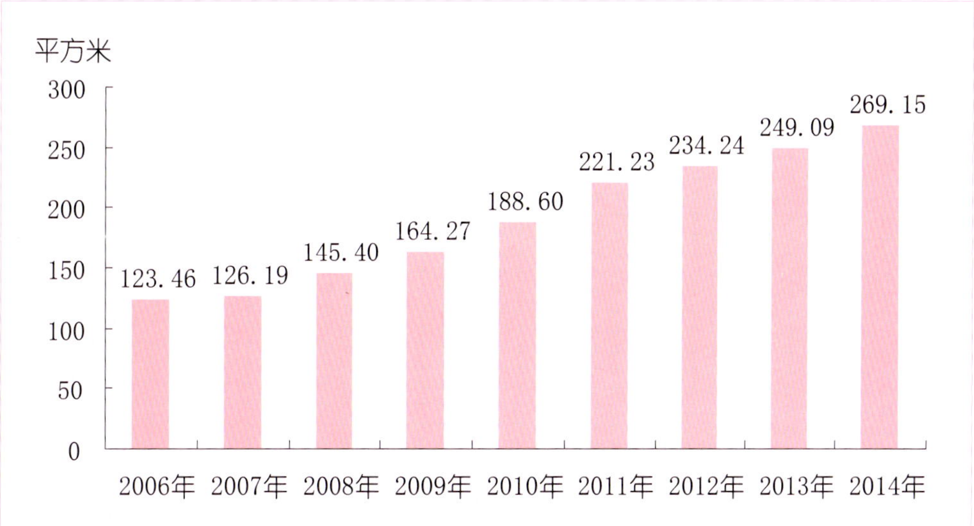

全年全国群众文化机构共组织开展各类活动[9]147.20万场次，比上年增长13.8%；服务人次50668万，增长14.7%。

表1　2014年全国群众文化机构开展活动情况

项　目	总量		比上年增长（%）	
	活动次数（万次）	参加人数（万人次）	活动次数	参加人次
各项活动总计	147.20	50668	13.8	14.7
#展览	13.17	10263	-4.7	11.0
文艺活动	84.54	36382	14.2	15.9
公益性讲座	2.56	445	8.1	0.9
训练班	46.93	3578	20.1	15.2

年末全国群众文化机构共有馆办文艺团体[10]6447个，演出13.34万场，观众8352万人次。由文化馆（站）指导的群众业余文艺团体40.46万个，馆办老年大学705个。

三、艺术创作演出

年末全国共有艺术表演团体[11]8769个，比上年末增加589个；从业人员26.29万人，增加0.20万人。其中各级文化部门管理的艺术表演团体2053个，占23.4%。

2014年，全国文艺表演团体坚持以人民为中心的创作导向，遵循文艺发展规律，牢固树立精品意识，以中国精神为灵魂，着力提高文艺作品的质量和水平。文化部通过开展“深入生活、扎根人民”主题实践活动，陆续组织近百批次上千名艺术家赴基层深入生活、采风创作、慰问演出，把人民作为文艺表现的主体，践行为人民抒写、为人民抒情、为人民抒怀的要求。全年全国艺术表演团体演出173.91万场，比上年增长5.3%；国内观众91020万人次，增长1.1%；赴农村演出114.04万场，增长8.5%，赴农村演出场次占总演出场次的65.6%，比重比上年增加2个百分点；农村观众55863万人次，比上年增长5.5%，占观众总人数的61.4%，比重比上年增加2.6个百分点。总收入226.40亿元，比上年下降19.1%，其中演出收入75.70亿元，比上年下降7.8%。

表2　2007年-2014年全国艺术表演团体基本情况

年　份	机构数（个）	从业人员数（人）	演出场次（万场）	国内演出观众人次（万人次）	营业总收入（万元）	
						#演出收入
2007年	4512	220653	92.7	75895.6	829045	203757
2008年	5114	208174	90.5	63186.8	933685	204842
2009年	6139	184678	120.2	81715.9	1121559	288214
2010年	6864	185413	137.1	88455.8	1239255	342696
2011年	7055	226599	154.7	74585.1	1540263	526745
2012年	7321	242047	135.0	82805.1	1968802	641480
2013年	8180	260865	165.1	90064.3	2800266	820738
2014年	8769	262887	173.9	91019.7	2264046	757028

全年全国文化部门所属艺术表演团体共组织政府采购的公益演出10.58万场，比上年增长18.3%；观众9893.36万人次，增长8.7%。利用流动舞台车演出10.62万场次，比上年增长5.9%；观众9900.64万人次，增长2.2%。

年末全国国有艺术表演场馆1338个，观众坐席数118.74万个。全年共举行艺术演出6.95万场，比上年增长5.3%，观众2598万人次，比上年下降2.4%。

四、文化产业与文化科技

2014年，文化部修订印发《国家文化产业示范基地管理办法》，开展第5批国家级文化产业示范（试验）园区和第6批国家文化产业示范基地申报评选命名工作。年末全国共有10个国家级文化产业示范园区，10个国家级文化产业试验园区和339个国家文化产业示范基地。建设国家文化产业项目服务平台，面向全国公开征集重点项目3834个。

文化部举办中国文化艺术政府奖第二届动漫奖，共评出30个奖项、80个入围项目。开展弘扬社会主义核心价值观动漫作品扶持计划，集中扶持革命传统教育、中华优秀传统文化主题的20个产品和42个创意项目。促进动漫与科技融合，深入推进手机（移动终端）动漫标准示范应用推广工程，开展标准修订工作，整合手机（移动终端）动漫运营平台。年末经文化部、财政部、国家税务总局三部门联合认定的动漫企业共有669个，重点动漫企业43个。

实施文化金融扶持计划，首次发布文化金融合作债券融资项目库，确定106个项目，获中央财政文化产业发展专项资金支持6.73亿元，比上年增长46%。推进文化产业信贷融资，年末全国文化产业本外币贷款余额1955亿元，同比增长30%以上。

2014年，文化部围绕文化重点工作，组织专项攻关，积极推动将文化领域的技术研发纳入国家科技创新体系，组织申报了3个国家科技支撑计划项目，申请国家资金4000余万元。加强文化科技创新载体建设，评定首批6家文化部重点实验室。完成2014年度国家文化科技提升计划、国家文化创新工程项目、文化部文化科技创新项目、文化部标准化制修订项目的申报、评审、立项、验收等工作。完成国家社科基金艺术学重大项目、年度项目等评审、立项、中期管理、鉴定结项工作，评审立项“文化部文化艺术科学研究项目”，强化艺术科研项目的对策研究，更好地为文化改革发展服务。

五、文化市场

年末全国文化市场经营单位[12]（含互联网上网服务营业场所、娱乐场所和民营艺术表演团体）22.00万个，比上年减少6541个；从业人员132.32万人，比上年减少12.86万人。全年全国文化市场经营单位营业收入1613.52亿元，比上年增长18.1%；营业利润468.06亿元，增长28.0%。

分区域看，年末城市文化市场经营单位77465个，占文化市场经营单位总量的35.2%；县城90453个，占41.1%;县以下地区52125个，占23.7%。

表3　2014年按区域全国文化市场经营单位主要指标

		机构数（个）	从业人员数（人）	营业总收入（万元）	利润总额（万元）
总量	总计	220043	1323248	16135167	4680616
	城市	77465	533590	8150929	2089175
	县城	90453	601410	4531994	1407732
	县以下	52125	188248	3452244	1183709
比重（%）	总计	100.0	100.0	100.0	100.0
	城市	35.2	40.3	50.5	44.6
	县城	41.1	45.4	28.1	30.1
	县以下	23.7	14.2	21.4	25.3

年末全国共有娱乐场所84137个，比上年末减少5515个；从业人员72.91万人，减少10.66万人；全年营业收入1101.87亿元，比上年增长24.6%；营业利润260.50亿元，增长17.1%。

年末全国共有互联网上网服务营业场所129289个，比上年末减少1724个；从业人员45.21万人，减少2.61万人；全年营业收入447.76亿元，比上年增长15.4%；营业利润196.20亿元，增长37.6%。

表4 2014年我国文化市场经营单位按业务分组情况

		机构数（个）	从业人员数（人）	营业总收入（万元）	利润总额（万元）
总量	总计	220043	1323248	16135167	4680616
	#娱乐场所	84137	729125	11018667	2604957
	互联网上网服务营业场所	129289	452105	4477597	1962040
比上年增长（%）	总计	-2.9	-8.9	18.1	33.1
	#娱乐场所	-6.2	-12.7	24.6	17.1
	互联网上网服务营业场所	-1.3	-5.5	15.4	37.6

六、文化遗产保护

年末全国共有文物机构8418个，比上年末增加681个。其中，文物保护管理机构3280个，占39.0%，博物馆[13]3658个，占43.5%。年末全国文物机构从业人员14.81万人，比上年末增加1.09万人。其中文物保护管理机构37843人，占25.6%；博物馆83970人，占56.7%。

图5 2006年-2014年全国文物机构及从业人员情况

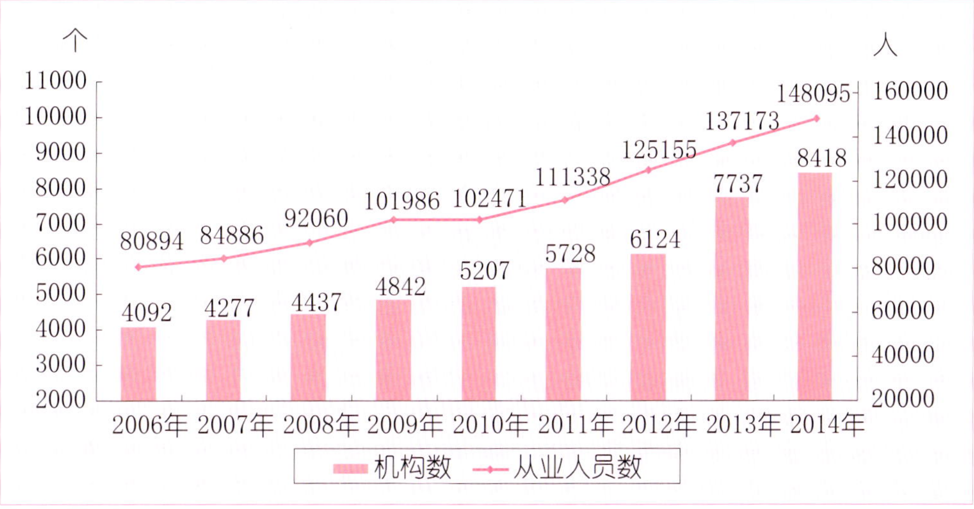

年末全国文物机构拥有文物藏品4063.58万件，比上年末增加222.77万件，增长5.8%。其中，博物馆文物藏品2929.97万件，占文物藏品总量的72.1%；文物商店文物藏品770.09万件，占18.9%。文物藏品中，一级文物9.82万件，占0.2%；二级文物68.82万件，占1.7%；三级文物340.51万件，占8.4%。

全年全国文物机构共安排基本陈列[14]9996个，比上年增长19.1%；举办临时展览[15]11174个，增长15.8%；接待观众84256万人次，增长12.8%。其中博物馆接待观众71774万人次，占文物机构接待观众总人次的85.2 %；文物保护管理机构接待观众12182万人次，占14.4%。参观人群中未成年人22403万人次，比上年增长10.7%占参观总人数的26.6%。

图6　2008年-2014年全国文物机构接待观众人次及未成年人观众人次

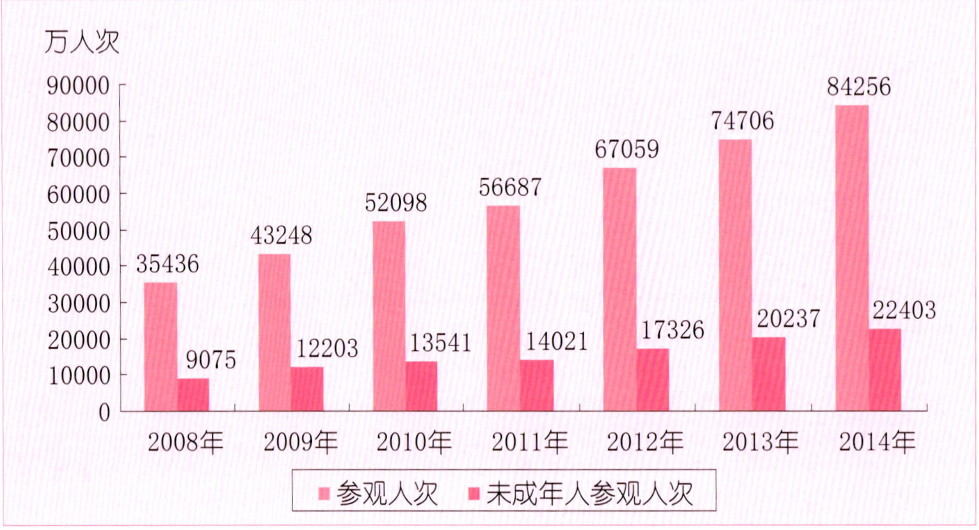

2014年，国务院公布第四批国家级非遗代表性项目153个、扩展项目153个。至此，国务院共公布了1372个国家级非物质文化遗产名录，文化部共认定了1986名国家级非物质文化遗产项目代表性传承人。据初步统计，年末全国共有非物质文化遗产保护机构[16]2645个，比上年增加120个；从业人员18692人，比上年增加564人。全年全国非物质文化遗产保护机构共举办展览16042次，接待观众3390万人次，分别比上年增长14.0%和9.9%；举办演出34703场，观众3795万人次，分别比上年增长31.8%和23.6%；举办民俗活动12982次，观众3884万人次，分别比上年增长5.0%和5.7%；举办培训班20946次，培训人数137万人次，分别比上年增长19.3%和13.2%。

七、对外和对港澳台文化交流

2014年，我国与21个国家签订或续签文化交流年度执行计划，与6个国家签订了互设文化中心协定和谅解备忘录；我国已签订的文化协定共计149个。全年经文化系统审批的对外文化交流项目

1667 起，40781 人次参加；对港澳文化交流项目 230 项，5593 人次参加；对台文化交流项目 500 项，12593 人次参加。

2014 年，文化部主动把对外文化工作放到国家外交整体战略中谋划定位。“欢乐春节”活动在 112 个国家和地区、321 个城市举办了 570 多项大型活动。圆满举办亚太经合组织第 22 次领导人非正式会议文艺演出、亚信峰会文艺晚会。组织开展庆祝中法建交五十周年音乐会、第十四届“相约北京”联欢活动等大型文化交流活动。积极践行“亲诚惠容”和“真实亲诚”理念，成功举办第五届中俄文化大集、首届“东亚文化之都”、2014 中国—东盟文化交流年、第二届中俄文化论坛、“中印友好交流年”等活动。

联合中国社科院共同举办了两期 2014“青年汉学家研修计划”，来自 39 个国家的 55 位青年汉学家应邀参加；举办“中国当代作品译介研修对接计划”，23 位海外青年汉学家、翻译家参加了研修；举办 2014“汉学与当代中国”座谈会，来自 17 个国家的 20 位外国前政要、知名学者和 14 位中方的杰出学者参会。

围绕中央战略部署，积极开展“一带一路”文化品牌的创立工作，成立“丝绸之路经济带西北五省区文化发展战略联盟”，举办首届“丝绸之路国际艺术节”、“海上丝绸之路国际艺术节”等一系列文化交流活动。

2014 年，文化部制定了《海外中国文化中心管理办法（试行）》及《海外中国文化中心评估框架》，为海外中国文化中心的健康运营提供了制度保障。2014 共完成 6 个海外文化中心的揭牌启用工作，海外文化中心总数达到 20 个。

2014 年，举办“艺海流金”、“港澳大学生文化实践活动”等活动，增强港澳各界对祖国的向心力。签署《粤港澳文化交流合作发展规划 2014-2018》，推进三地文化与区域建设的共同发展。打造“艺传两岸—台湾青少年中华传统文化培训”等对台青年文化交流品牌。依托“第七届海峡两岸文博会”等平台，推动两岸文化产业对接与合作。

八、文化资金投入

2014 年，中央财政通过继续实施“三馆一站”免费开放、非遗保护、公共数字文化建设、地市级公共文化设施建设等中央补助地方文化项目，共落实中央补助地方专项资金 46.53 亿元，比上年增长 0.72%。

图 7　2006 年 -2014 年中央对地方文化项目补助资金情况

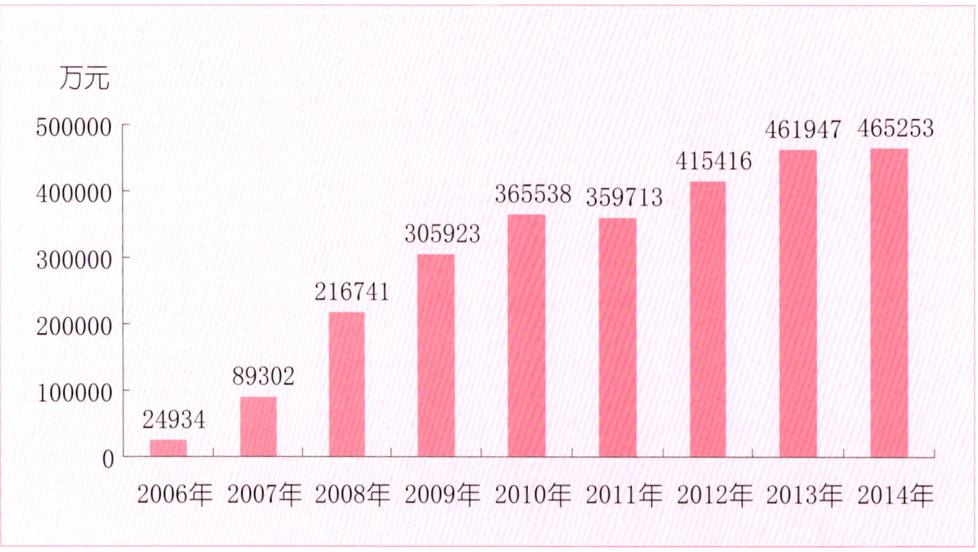

全年全国文化事业费[17]583.44 亿元，比上年增加 52.95 亿元，增长 10.0%；全国人均文化事业费 42.65 元，比上年增加 3.66 元，增长 9.4%。

图 8　2000 年 -2014 年全国人均文化事业费

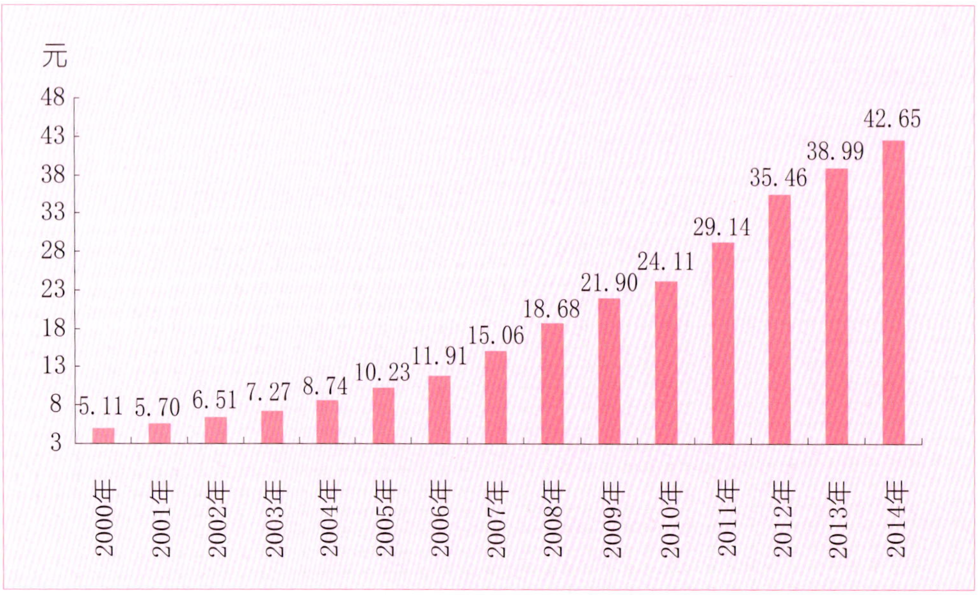

全国文化事业费占财政总支出的比重为 0.38%，与上年基本持平。

图 9　全国文化事业费占财政总支出比重

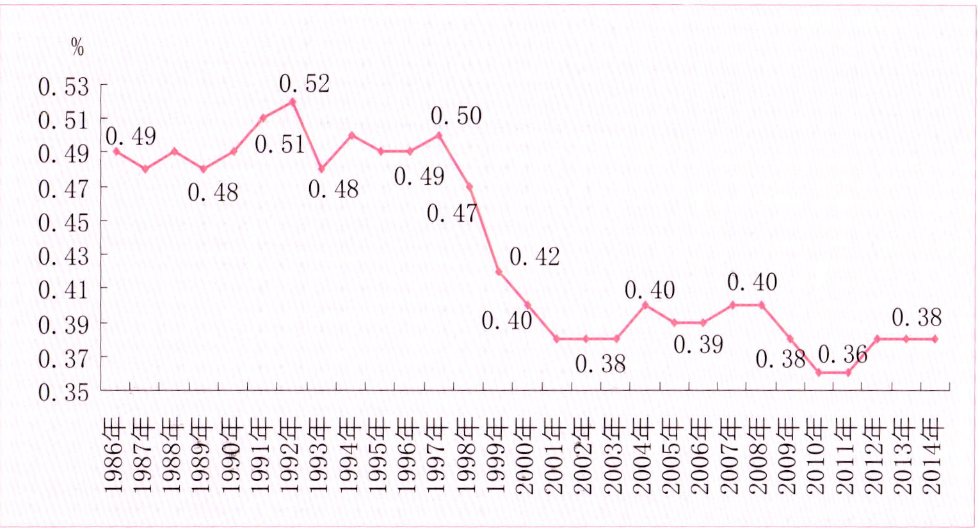

全国文化事业费中，县以上文化单位 292.12 亿元，占 50.1%，比重比上年降低了 1.3 个百分点；县及县以下文化单位 291.32 亿元，占 49.9%，比重比上年提高了 1.3 个百分点。东部地区[18]文化单位文化事业费 242.98 亿元，占 41.6%，比重比上年下降了 2.0 个百分点；中部地区文化单位文化事业费 133.46 亿元，占 22.9%，比重提高了 0.3 个百分点；西部地区文化单位文化事业费 171.15 亿元，占 29.3%，比重提高了 0.6 个百分点。

表 5　全国文化事业费按城乡和区域分布情况

项　目		1995 年	2000 年	2005 年	2010 年	2012 年	2013 年	2014 年
总量（亿元）	全　国	33.39	63.16	133.82	323.06	480.10	530.49	583.44
	#县以上	24.44	46.33	98.12	206.65	243.08	272.67	292.12
	县及县以下	8.95	16.87	35.70	116.41	237.02	257.82	291.32
	#东部地区	13.43	28.85	64.37	143.35	211.56	231.41	242.98
	中部地区	9.54	15.05	30.58	78.65	107.78	120.01	133.46
	西部地区	8.30	13.70	27.56	85.78	139.53	152.16	171.15
所占比重（%）	全　国	100.0	100.0	100.0	100.0	100.0	100.0	100.0
	#县以上	73.2	73.4	73.3	64.0	50.6	51.4	50.1
	县及县以下	26.8	26.7	26.7	36.0	49.4	48.6	49.9
	#东部地区	40.2	45.7	48.1	44.4	44.1	43.6	41.6
	中部地区	28.6	23.8	22.9	24.3	22.4	22.6	22.9
	西部地区	24.9	21.7	20.6	26.6	29.1	28.7	29.3

全国文物事业费[19]247.87 亿元，比上年增加 16.12 亿元，增长 7.0%；文物事业费占财政总支出的比重为 0.17%，比重与上年基本持平。

据财政部统计，2014 年全国财政支出中，文化体育传媒经费[20]2753 亿元，比上年增长 9.2%，占财政支出的 1.82%，比重与上年基本持平。

图 10　2006 年 -2014 年全国文化体育传媒经费总量及增长速度

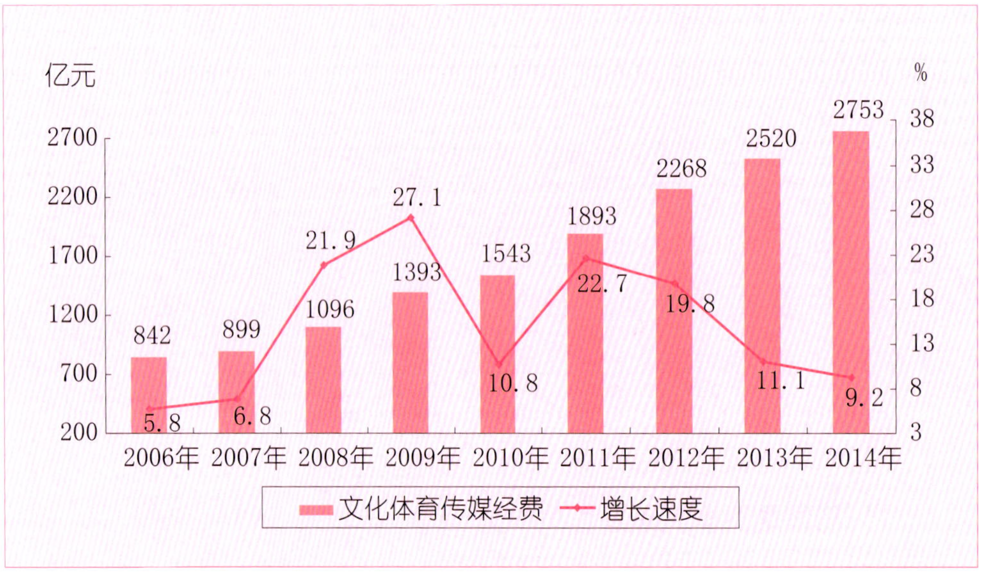

注释:

[1] 本公报中各项统计数据均未包括香港特别行政区、澳门特别行政区和台湾省。部分数据因四舍五入的原因，存在着与分项合计不等的情况。

[2] 文化单位是指全国各级文化部门(含文化系统和文物系统)主办的或实行行业管理的文化机构，不含各级新闻出版、广播影视等部门主办或管理的文化机构。根据现行的统计制度，文化部门主办的文化单位（如公共图书馆、文化馆、文化站、博物馆等）全部纳入了统计范围，实行行业管理的文化单位中，民营艺术表演团体、互联网上网服务营业场所和娱乐场所纳入了统计范围，艺术品交易机构、网络文化经营机构等未纳入统计范围。

[3] 从业人员是指在各级文化部门（含文化系统和文物系统）主办或实行行业管理的机构中工作并取得劳动报酬的人员。统计范围同文化单位。

[4] 公共图书馆是指由各级文化部门主办的、面向社会公众开放并提供科学、文化等各种知识普及教育的机构。

[5] 公共图书馆总藏量指已编目的古籍、图书、期刊和报纸的合订本、手册、手稿，以及缩微制品、录像带、录音带、光盘等视听文献资料数量之和，不包括电子图书。

[6] 公共图书馆发放的借书证数是指由公共图书馆发放，并在当年内使用过至少一次的借书证数。

[7] 公共图书馆总流通人次是指本年度内到图书馆场馆接受图书馆服务的总人次，包括借阅书刊、咨询问题，以及参加各类读者活动等。

[8] 群众文化机构是指各级文化部门主办的开展群众文化活动的场所，主要包括文化馆（含综合性文化中心、群众艺术馆）、文化站。

[9] 群众文化机构组织开展活动是指组织文艺活动、举办训练班、举办展览和组织公益性讲座总和。

[10] 群众文化机构馆办文艺团体指由本馆人员组成的为群众提供文艺演出的演出团队。

[11] 艺术表演团体指由文化部门主办或实行行业管理（经文化行政部门审批并领取营业性演出许可证），专门从事表演艺术等活动的各类专业艺术表演团体。

[12] 文化市场经营单位指经文化市场行政部门审批或备案并领取相关许可或备案文件的、从事文化经营和文化服务活动的机构。按照现行统计制度，文化市场经营单位统计范围只包括民营艺术表演团体、娱乐场所和互联网上网服务营业场所。

[13] 博物馆指为了研究、教育、欣赏的目的，收藏、保护、展示人类活动和自然环境的见证物，向公众开放，非营利性、永久性社会服务机构，包括以博物馆（院）、纪念馆（舍）、科技馆、陈列馆等专有名称开展活动的单位。

[14] 基本陈列指在本馆布置陈列、地点固定、时间较长的展出。

[15] 临时展览指在本机构内设置，由本馆设计布陈，形式比较多样的展出。

[16] 非物质文化遗产保护机构是指各级非物质文化遗产保护中心或非物质文化遗产保护办公室。

[17] 文化事业费是指区域内各级财政对文化系统主办单位的经费投入总和。一般包括艺术表演团体、公共图书馆、文化馆（站）等文化事业单位的财政拨款（不含基建拨款）及文化部门所属企业的财政补贴。根据现行统计口径，文化事业费不包括各级文化行政管理部门的行政运行经费。

[18] 东部地区包括北京、天津、辽宁、上海、江苏、浙江、福建、山东、广东；中部地区包括河北、山西、吉林、黑龙江、安徽、江西、河南、湖北、湖南、海南；西部地区包括内蒙古、广西、重庆、四川、贵州、云南、西藏、陕西、甘肃、青海、宁夏、新疆。

[19] 文物事业费是指区域内各级财政对文物事业的经费投入总和。一般包括博物馆、文物保护管理机构等文物事业单位的财政拨款（不含基建拨款）及文物部门所属企业的财政补贴。

[20] 文化体育传媒经费数据源自财政部，是指各级政府在文化、文物、体育、广播影视和新闻出版方面的投入。

Statistical Communiqué of the Ministry of Culture of the People's Republic of China on Cultural Development in 2014[1]

In 2014, all government cultural departments in China have implemented and put into practice the spirit of the 18th CPC National Congress, the 3rd and the 4th Plenary Session of 18th CPC Central Committee, and studied and drew on the essence of important speeches made by Chinese President Xi Jinping in an in-depth way. With the aim to build a culturally strong socialist China, nurture and promote the core socialist values, and serve the interests of the people, they worked hard with responsible, practical, realistic and active approaches and made various new breakthroughs and progresses in all fields of work.

1. Institution and Employment

287,400 national cultural units[2] were brought into the statistical range by the end of 2014, 5,500 less than that of the previous year; the number of employees[3] was 2.0402 million, 114,700 persons less than previous year. Among them, 65,600 units were affiliated to government cultural departments, 872 more than those of the past year, with 638,200 employees, almost the same with the number of the past year.

Figure 1: Number of china's cultural units and employees in 2006-2014

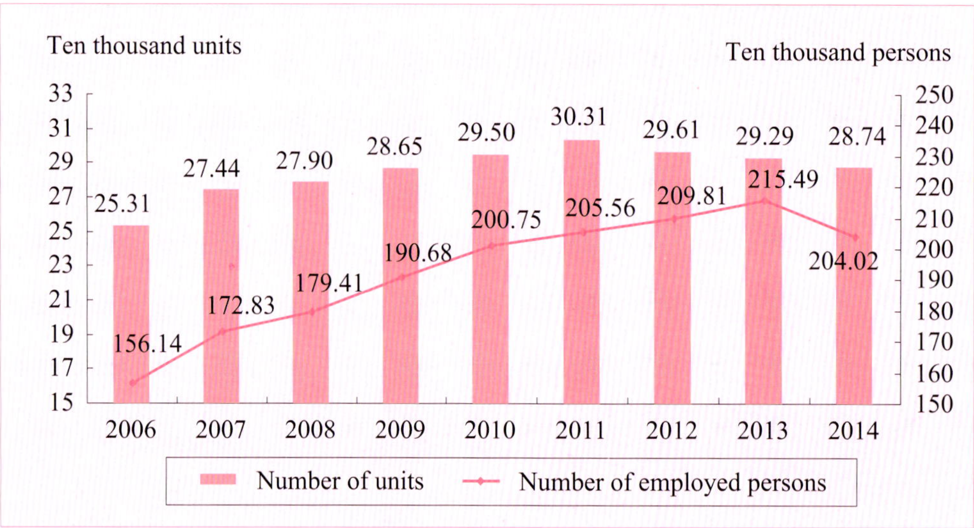

2. Public Cultural Service System

In 2014, the Ministry of Culture took the leading role in forming the coordination team for building the national public cultural services system of China on the basis of mutual consultations, and integrated and comprehensive working approaches. The Opinion on Accelerating the Building of A Modern Public Cultural Services System and the National Guiding Benchmarks for Basic Public Cultural Services were drafted, which specified the constitutional structure of China's modern public cultural services system and provided substantial support for the growth of public cultural undertakings in China.

(1) Public Libraries[4]

By the end of the year, there were in total 3,117 libraries nationwide, 5 more than the number of the previous year. Among them, children's libraries were 108, an increase of 3. The total number of employees of public libraries across China reached 56,071, among which 5,479 owned senior professional titles, accounting for 9.8%, and 18,146 owned medium-level professional titles, accounting for 32.4%.

According to statistics at the end of 2014, the actual floor space used by public library buildings totaled 12,316,000m^2, up by 6.3% over the end of the previous year. 79.092 million books[5] and 50,674 E-books were collected in these libraries, up by 5.6% and 34.2% respectively. The number of seats in reading rooms was 855,500, up by 5.7%, and that of computers was 198,600, up by 1.6%, and that of electronic reading terminals for readers was 121,600, up by 4.6%.

By the end of the 2014 the area of structure of public libraries for each ten thousand persons was 90 m^2, an increase of 4.9 m^2 over the end of the previous year; the number of books per capita was 0.58, an increase of 0.03 over the previous year; the money spent on books per capita was 1.24 yuan, an increase of 0.02 yuan over previous year.

Figure 2: Information of per capita resource of national public libraries in 2006-2014

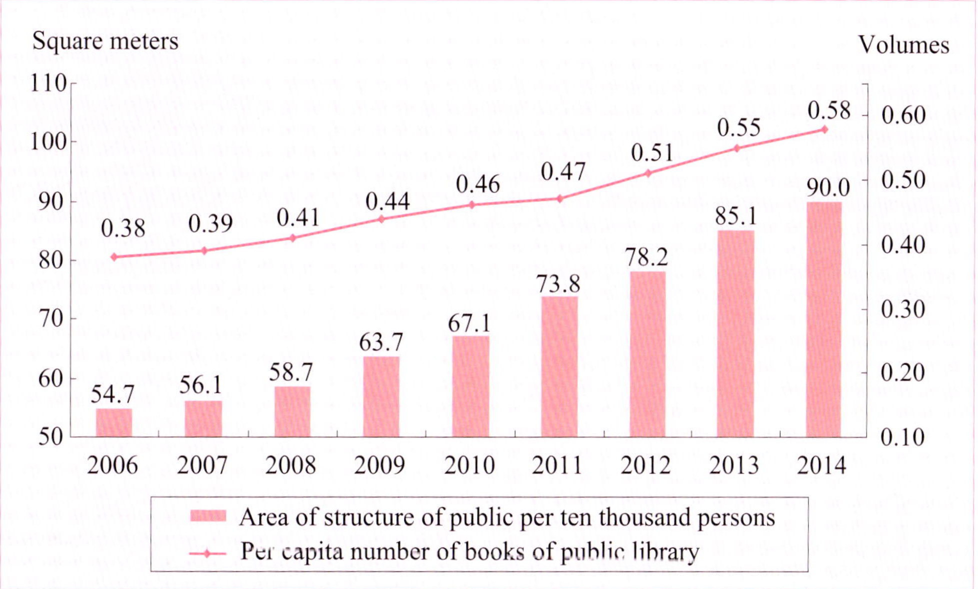

The library cards[6] the national public libraries handed out all through the year numbered 39.44 million, up by 37.1% over the previous year; the total flow of person-time[7] reached 530.36 million, a growth of 7.7%. A total number of times that books, magazines and documents were lent out reached 467.34 million, up by 14.4%; a total of 227.37 million persons borrowed books, a growth of 10.6%. Various activities organized for readers totaled 103,586, up by 13.2%; and the number of participants reached 50.15 million, an increase of 13.7%.

Figure 3: Total flow of person-time and number of books lent out of national public libraries in 2006-2014

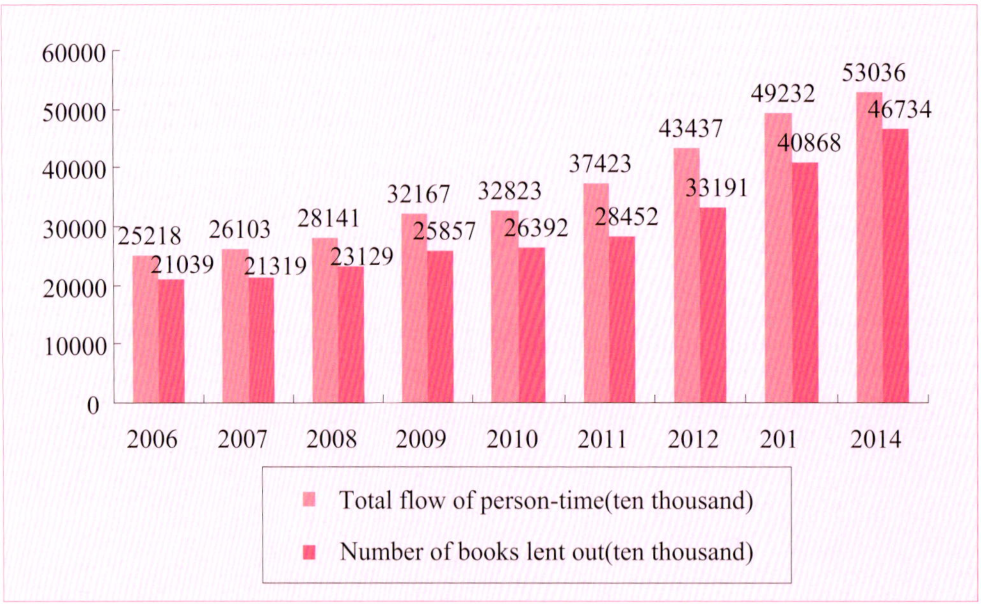

(2) Public and community Cultural Institutions[8]

There were a total of 44,423 cultural institutions for mass public across the country by the end of 2014, an increase of 163 over the end of the previous year. Among them, comprehensive cultural stations in townships numbered 34,465, a growth of 122. By the end of the year the persons employed by cultural institutions for mass public nationwide reached 170,299, an increase of 5,944 over the end of the previous year. The staff with senior professional title reached 5,633, accounting for 3.3%; and the number of staff with medium-level professional title was 16,605, accounting for 9.8%.

By the end of the year the floor space of buildings actually used was 36,863,390 m^2, up by 8.8% over the end of the previous year; the number of book collections was 248 million, up by 7.8%; that of computers was 346,700, up by 18.6%; the area of reading rooms opened to the public was 1.0802 million m^2, up by 8.3%. By then end of the year the area of structure of cultural facilities of mass for each ten thousand persons was 269.51 m^2, an increase of 20.42 m^2 over the end of previous year.

Figure 4: Area of structure of national cultural facilities of mass per ten thousand people in 2006-2014

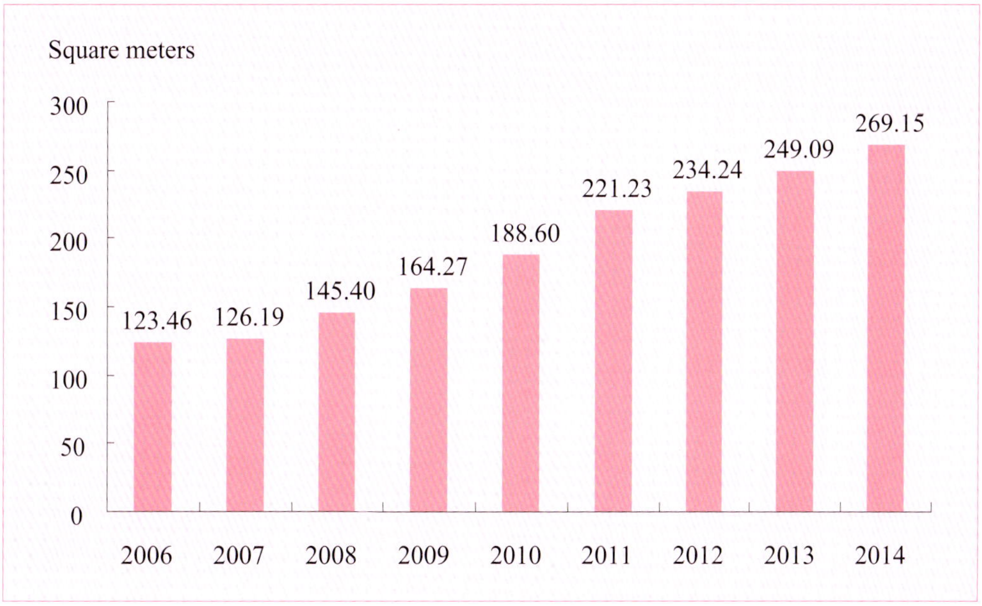

The number of activities[9] all year round organized by the nationwide cultural institutions for the mass public was 1,472,000, up by 14.7% over the previous year; that of people served was 506.58 million, up by 14.7%.

Information of activities implemented by nationwide cultural institutions for mass public in 2014

	Gross		Increase over previous year (%)	
	Number of activity (ten thousand)	Number of participants (ten thousand person-time)	Number of activity	Person-time of participant
Aggregate of activities	**147.20**	**50654**	**13.8**	**14.7**
#Exhibition	13.17	10263	-4.7	11.0
Cultural activities	84.54	36372	14.2	15.9
Public lecture	2.56	445	8.5	0.9
Training class	46.93	3578	20.1	15.2

By the end of the year the nationwide cultural institutions totally had 6,447 cultural-center-based art groups[10] founded by city or township cultural centers, which had given 133,400 performances for 83.52 million spectators. The number of amateur cultural-center-based art groups were guided by cultural centers (stations) was 404,600, and that of university for the elderly set up by cultural centers was 705.

3. Performing Arts

By the end of the year art performance troupes[11] reached 8,769, an increase of 589 over the end of the previous year; that of the employed people reached 262,900 with the increase of 2000. Of them, the art performance troupes managed by cultural departments at all levels reached 2,053, accounting for 23.4%.

In 2014, the art performing troupes of China has kept working for the people, endeavored to present more brilliant productions with the soul of Chinese spirit. By conducting the "Taking Root in the Life of the People" project, the Ministry of Culture of China organized more than 1,000 artists in about 100 groups to visit grassroot communities, write new works about them and present performances for them, putting the people on the center stage in their works, depicting the people's life, emotions and aspirations.

In 2014, all art troupes in China presented 1.7391 million performances, an increase of 5.3% over the previous year; the domestic audiences reached 910.2 million, up by 1.1%; the number of performances for rural areas was 1,140,400, up by 8.5%, accounting for 65.6% of total number; that of the rural audiences was 558.63 million, up by 5.5% and accounting for 61.4% of overall number of audiences, up by 2.6 percentage points over that of the previous year. The total turnover of the performing troupes was 22.64 billion yuan, a decrease of 19.1% over the previous year; of them the income from performances was 7,57 billion yuan, down by 7.8%.

Table 2: General information of art troupes nationwide in 2007-2014

Year	Number of institutions	Number of employed people	Number of performances (ten thousand)	Number of audiences for domestic performance (ten thousand)	Total income (ten thousand yuan)	
						#Income from performance
2007	4512	220653	92.7	75895.6	829045	203757
2008	5114	208174	90.5	63186.8	933685	204842
2009	6139	184678	120.2	81715.9	1121559	288214
2010	6864	185413	137.1	88455.8	1239255	342696
2011	7055	226599	154.7	74585.1	1540263	526745
2012	7321	242047	135.0	82805.1	1968802	641480
2013	8180	260865	165.1	90064.3	2800266	735532
2014	8769	262887	173.9	91019.7	2264048	757028

The amount of govermment-purchased public performances presented by art performance troupes directly administered by cultural departments throughout the year was 105,800, 18.3% increase over the number of the previous year, with audiences of 98.9336 million, up by 8.7%. The number of the performances on travelling stage vans was 106,200, with audiences of 99.0064 million, up by 5.9% and 2.2% respectively.

By the end of the year, the state-owned venues of the performing arts amounted to 1,338, with 1,187,400 seats. 69,500 performances were held throughout the year, up by 5.3% over the previous year; the audiences reached 25.98 million, a decrease of 2.4%.

4. Cultural Industry, Science and Technology

In 2014, the Ministry of Culture of China revised and published the Regulations for National Role Model Bases for Cultural Industry, launched the application, deliberation and authorization of the 5th batch of the National Role Model (Pilot) Parks for Cultural Industry and the 6th batch of the National Role Model Bases for Cultural Industry. By the end of 2014, there were in total 10 National Role Model Parks for Cultural Industry, 10 National Pilot Parks for Cultural Industry and 339 National Cultural Industry Role Model Bases. The national cultural industry service platform was established with 3834 key projects open for national bidding.

The Ministry of Culture of China has given 30 prizes and 80 qualified contestants as it hosted the 2nd Cartoon and Animation Awards under the umbrella of China's government awards for culture and arts. It also launched the supporting program for cartoon and animation works that illustrated socialist core values, and focused its support on 20 products and 42 creative items for revolution tradition education and the essence of Chinese traditional culture. The Ministry of Culture also facilitated the integration of cartoon, animation and technology, substantially promoted the role model APPs of cartoon and animation on handheld devices, revised the benchmarks to integrate the operating platforms on mobile phones and handheld devices. By the end of 2014, there were in total 669 cartoon and animation enterprises authorized by the Ministry of Culture, Ministry of Finance and the State Administration of Taxation, among them 43 were major ones.

The financial support program for culture was launched, releasing for the first time the financing projects database for cultural and financial cooperation bonds, in which 106 projects were authorized. In total, the program received 673 million yuan from the cultural industry special fund in the central budget of China, up by 46 % over that of the previous year. Credit financing for cultural industry was boosted, and the national balance of the RMB and foreign currency loan has exceeded 190 billion yuan, up by more than 30% than that of the previous year.

In 2014, the Ministry of Culture of Culture focused on the major work in cultural areas, targeted the special challenges and actively facilitated the inclusion of technology R&D in cultural fields into the national system for technological innovation. The Ministry of Culture organized the application of 3 items for national technology supporting program, applying for more than 40 million yuan of national fund. The vessels for cultural technology innovations were built, 6 key laboratories authorized by the Ministry of Culture of China were identified. The application, deliberation, identification and review of cultural science and technology upgrading program in 2014 were accomplished, as well as those of the national cultural innovation program, cultural technology innovation program of the Ministry of Culture, and the benchmark establishment and revision program. The deliberation, authorization, management, identification and review for the major and annual programs of the art theory category of the National Social Science Fund were completed.

The Cultural and Arts Science Research Program of the Ministry of Culture of China was evaluated, reviewed and established to strengthen the research for art strategies and better serve the cultural reform and development of China.

5. Cultural Market

At the end of the year the operating units[12] (including business sites of internet access services, entertainment venues and private art performance troupes) of the national cultural market reached 220,000, 6541 less than those of the previous year, with 1,323,200 employees, 128,600 less than those of the previous year. Throughout the year, the turnover of units of national cultural markets reached 161.352 billion yuan, and their gross profit was 46.806 billion yuan, increasing by 18.1% and 28% respectively over the numbers of the previous year.

By the end of 2014, the number of operating units of urban cultural markets was 77,465, accounting for 35.2% of total operating units of cultural markets; that of county was 90,453, and accounted for 41.1%; and areas smaller than county 52,125, accounting for 23.7%.

Table 3: Key indicators for operating units of national cultural markets according to area in 2014

		Number of institutions	Employed people	Gross revenue (ten thousand yuan)	Gross profit (ten thousand yuan)
Amount	**Aggregate**	**220043**	**1323248**	**16135167**	**4680616**
	City	77465	533590	8150929	2089175
	County	90453	601410	4531994	1407732
	Areas lower than county	52125	188248	3452244	1183709
Proportion (%)	**Aggregate**	**100.0**	**100.0**	**100.0**	**100.0**
	City	35.2	40.3	50.5	44.6
	County	41.1	45.4	28.1	30.1
	Areas lower than county	23.7	14.2	21.4	25.3

By the end of the year the number of entertainment venues went to 84,137, a decrease of 5515; the number of employees was 729,100, a decrease of 106,600; the annual revenue was 110.187 billion yuan, up by 24.6% over the previous year; profit was 26.05 billion yuan, up by 17.1% over the previous year.

By the end of the year, there were 129,289 businesses of internet access services across the country, a decrease of 1,724 over the end of the previous year; the number of employees was 452,100, an decrease of 26,100; the annual turnover was 44.776 billion yuan, up by 15.4%, with profit of 19.621 billion yuan, up by 37.6%.

Table 4: Business based operating agencies of national cultural markets in 2014

		Number of institution	Employed people	Gross revenue (ten thousand yuan)	Total profit (ten thousand yuan)
Amount	**Aggregate**	**220043**	**1323248**	**16135167**	**4680616**
	#entertainment venue	84137	729125	11018667	2604957
	Business sites of internet access service	129289	452105	4477597	1962040
Increase over previous year(%)	**Aggregate**	**-2.9**	**-8.9**	**18.1**	**33.1**
	#entertainment venue	-6.2	-12.7	24.6	17.1
	Business sites of internet access service	-1.3	-5.5	15.4	37.6

6. Cultural Heritage Safeguarding

By the end of the year there were 8,418 cultural heritage institutions, an increase of 681 over the end of the previous year. Of them 3,280 were for preservation of cultural heritage, accounting for 39%, and 3,658 were museums[13], accounting for 43.5%. By the end of the year the number of employees in cultural heritage institutions was 148,100, an increase of 10,900 over that of the end of the previous year. The people working in agencies for preservation of cultural heritage reached 37,843, accounting for 25.6%; and that in museums numbered 83,970, accounting for 56.7%.

Figure 5: Information of national cultural relics agencies and employed persons in 2006-2014

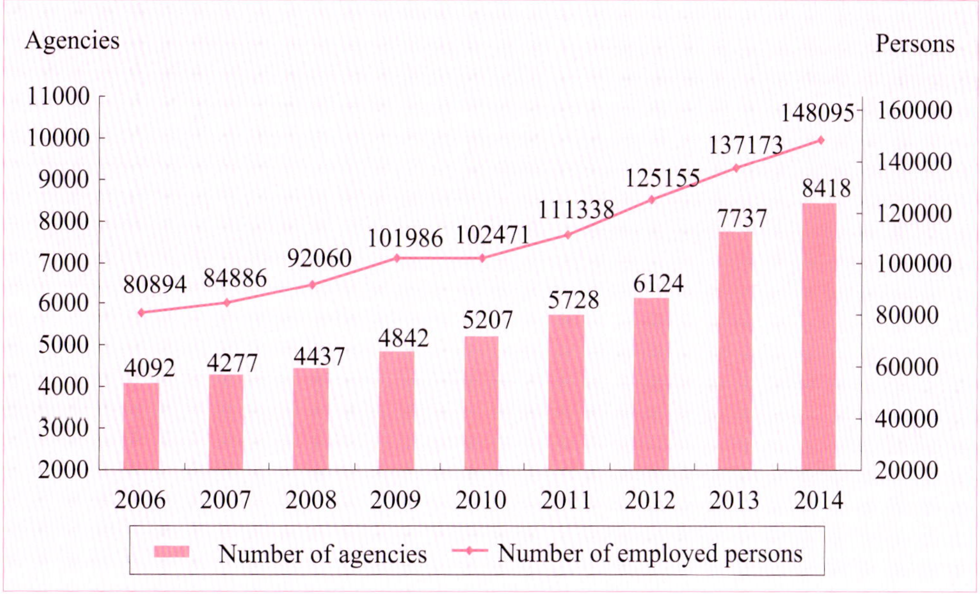

By the end of the year there were 40.6358 million pieces of cultural relics in cultural heritage institutions, an increase of 2.2277 million over the end of the previous year or up by 5.8%. Of them, the amount collected by museums was 29.2997 million, accounting for 72.1% of the total number; that of heritage shops was 7.7009 million, accounting for 18.9%. Among those collections, the amount of grade-one cultural relics was 98,200, accounting for 0.2%; that of grade-two cultural relics 688,200, accounting for 1.7%; that of grade-three cultural relics 3,405,100, accounting for 8.4%.

Throughout the year the permanent exhibitions[14] arranged by cultural heritage institutions reached 9,996 and temporary exhibitions[15] totaled 11,174, with 842,56 million visitor attendances, an increase of 12.8%. Of them, the number of visitors to museums was 717.44 million, accounting for 85.2% of total number of visitors to cultural heritage institutions; that to cultural heritage safeguarding institutions was 121.82 million, accounting for 14.4%. Among the visitors, the number of minors was 224.03 million, up by 10.7%, accounting for 26.6% of total visitors.

Figure 6: Person-time of audiences and minors cultural relic agencies accepting in 2008-2014

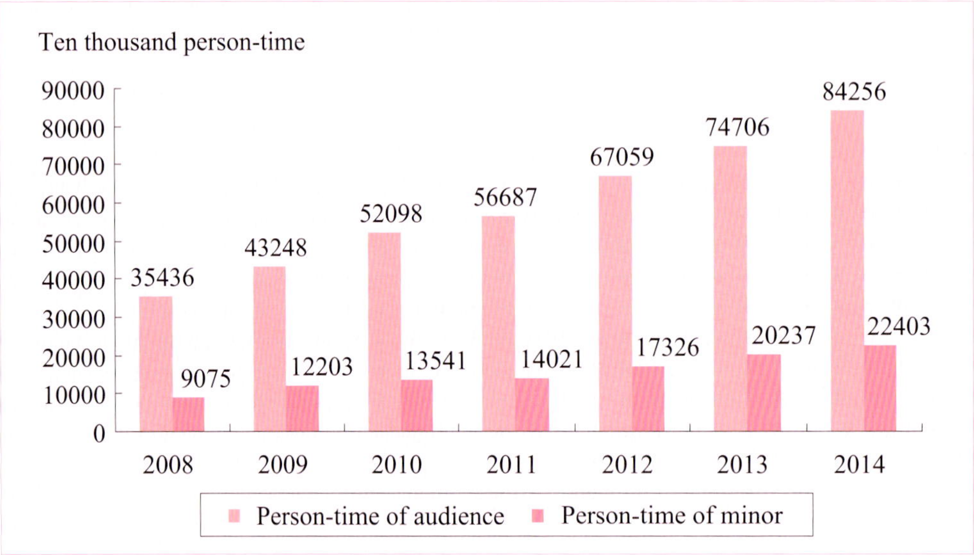

In 2014, after adding the fourth batch of intangible cultural heritage items, which were 153 and 153 extended items, the Ministry of Culture has identified a total of 1,372 state-level lists of the intangible cultural heritage and 1,986 representative inheritors of state-level intangible cultural heritage items. According to preliminary survey there were 2,645 intangible cultural heritage safeguarding institutions[16], with 18,692 employees by the end of the year, increasing by 120 and 564 respectively. The a intangible cultural heritage safeguarding institutions held 16,042 exhibitions throughout the year with 33.90 million visitor attendances, up by 14% and 9.9% than that of the previous year respectively; the number of performances that they held was 34,703 with 37.95 million audience attendances; that of folk lore activities 12,982 with audiences of 38.84 million audience attendances, up by 5% and 5.7 % over that of the previous year; that of training classes 20,946 with trainees of 1.37 million person-times, up by 19.3% and 13.2% over that of the previous year respectively.

7. Cultural Exchange with Foreign Countries and Cultural Bonding with Hong Kong, Macao and Taiwan Regions

In 2014, China has signed or renewed annual executive programs with 21 foreign countries, and signed agreements or MOUs on the mutual establishment of cultural centers with 6 countries. So far, China has signed 149 cultural agreements with other countries. Throughout the year, there were 1,667 external cultural exchange programs authorized by all levels of cultural authorities, with 40,781 participant attendances. There were 230 cultural interaction programs with Hong Kong and Macao, with 5,593 participants and 500 with Taiwan, with 12,593 participants.

In 2014, the Ministry of Culture of China spontaneously planned external cultural programs in conformity with China's comprehensive diplomatic strategy. The Happy Chinese New Year program toured 321 cities in 112 countries and regions presenting more than 570 major activities. The cultural galas and music concerts to celebrate the 22nd APEC Informal Leaders' Meeting, the CICA Summit, the 50th anniversary of the establishment of diplomatic relations between China and France, and the 14th Meet in Beijing Arts Festival. The Ministry of Culture actively put the ideas of amity, sincerity, mutual benefit, inclusiveness and true results into action in conducting cultural exchange, and successfully held the China-Russia Cultural Bazaar, first Cultural Capital of East Asia program, 2014 China-ASEAN Year of Cultural Exchange, the 2nd China-Russia Cultural Forum, as well as the China-India Year of Friendly Exchange.

The Ministry of Culture joined hands with the Chinese Academy of Social Sciences in holding two sessions of 2014 Workshop for Young Sinologists, with the participation of 55 young sinologists from 39 countries. The Ministry of Culture also held the program for the research, translation and promotion of contemporary Chinese literature with the participation of 23 foreign translators and young sinologists, as well as the 2014 Seminar on Sinologists and Contemporary China, attended by 20 foreign former political figures and renowned scholars and 14 established Chinese scholars.

The Ministry of Culture of China, in accordance with the strategic plan of the central government, actively engaged in fostering flagship cultural events for the Belt and Road Initiatives, established the Cultural Development Strategy Alliance for Five Northwestern Provinces and Autonomous Regions on the Silk Road Economic Belt, held cultural events including the first Silk Road International Arts Festival and the Maritime Silk Road International Arts Festival.

In 2014, the Ministry of Culture of China formulated the Overseas China Cultural Centers Regulations (draft) and the Framework Deliberation Benchmarks for Overseas China Cultural Centers, providing institutional guarantee for sustainable functioning of overseas China cultural centers. In 2014, 6 new overseas China cultural centers were opened, and the total number of overseas China cultural centers reached 20.

In 2014, the Ministry of Culture of China held visiting programs for Hong Kong and Macao cultural and art professionals as well as for university students to increase the cohesiveness of the Chinese mainland, Hong Kong and Macao. The Cultural Bonding and Cooperation Development Plan between Guangdong Province, Hong Kong and Macao from 2014-2018 was signed to boost the cohesive progress of these three localities in cultural fields at regional level. Programs including the Chinese traditional culture training program for children and young people in Taiwan were conducted for Taiwan, and with the support of platforms including the 7th Cross-Straits Cultural Industries Fair, the Ministry of Culture facilitated the cultural bonding and cooperation between Chinese mainland and Taiwan.

8. Financial Investment in Culture

In 2014, the central budget of China continued to subsidize local culture by implementing cultural projects, such as free access to museums, libraries, and cultural centers (stations). It provided special funding in total 4,653 million yuan, up by 0.72% over that of the previous year.

Figure 7: Information of subvention of central authority to local cultural projects in 2006-2014

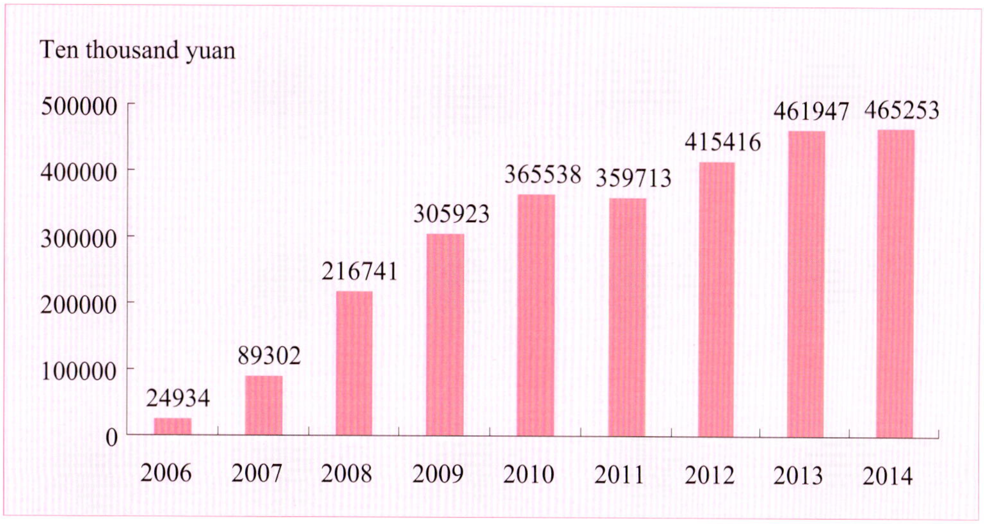

The total amount of cultural undertaking expenses[17] all across the country in 2014 was 58.344 billion yuan, an increase of 5.295 billion yuan over the previous year, up by 10%; that of the national cultural undertaking expenses per capita was 42.65 yuan, an increase of 3.66 yuan over previous year, up by 9.4%.

Figure 8: Information of cultural operating expenses per capita in 2000-2014

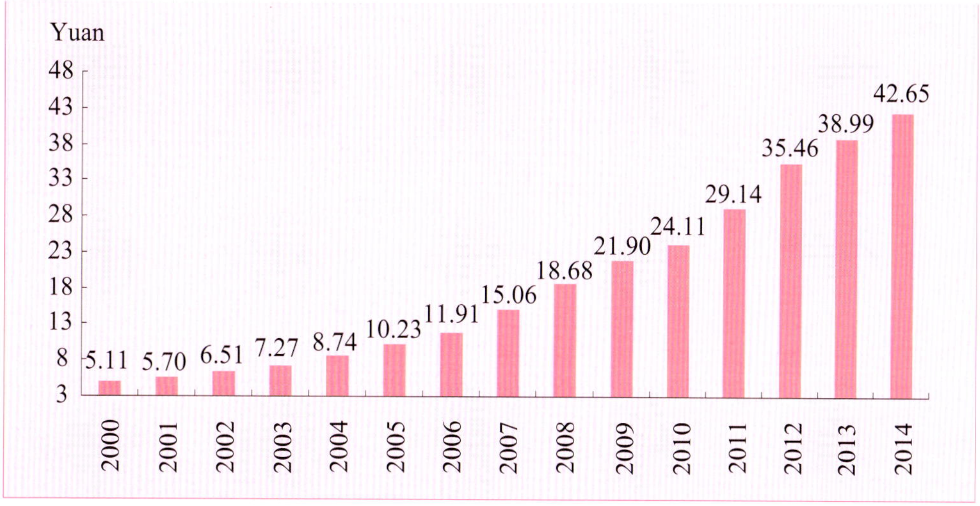

The national cultural undertaking expenses accounted for 0.38% of the country's total financial expenditure, and the proportion was basically the same with the previous year.

Figure 9: Proportion of national cultural operating expense in financial expenditure

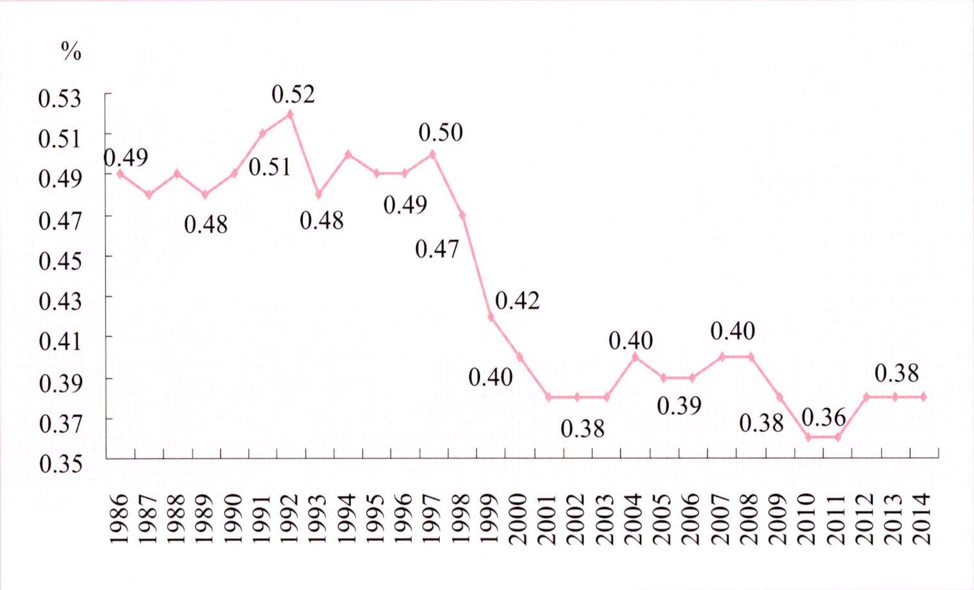

Regarding the national cultural undertaking expenses, that of cultural units above county level was 29.212 billion yuan, accounting for 50.1%, 1.3 percentage points down than that of the previous year; that of cultural units of county level or below the level of county was 29.132 billion yuan, accounting for 49.9%, and the proportion increased by 1.3% from the previous year. The cultural undertaking expenses of eastern region[18] reached 24.298 billion yuan, accounting for 41.6%, and its proportion decreased by 2%; that of central region 13.346 billion yuan, accounting for 22.9%, its proportion increased by 0.3%; and that of western region 17.115 billion yuan, accounting for 29.3%, its proportion increased by 0.6%.

Table 5: Urban & rural and regional-based distribution of national cultural operating expenses

		In 1995	In 2000	In 2005	In 2010	In 2012	In 2013	In 2014
Aggregate (one hundred million yuan)	Nationwide	33.39	63.16	133.82	323.06	480.10	530.49	583.44
	# above county level	24.44	46.33	98.12	206.65	243.08	272.67	292.12
	County level and below level of county	8.95	16.87	35.70	116.41	237.02	257.82	291.32
	# Eastern region	13.43	28.85	64.37	143.35	211.56	231.41	242.98
	Central region	9.54	15.05	30.58	78.65	107.78	120.01	133.46
	Western region	8.30	13.70	27.56	85.78	139.53	152.16	171.15
Proportion (%)	Nationwide	100.0	100.0	100.0	100.0	100.0	100.0	100.0
	# above county level	73.2	73.4	73.3	64.0	50.6	51.4	50.1
	County level and below level of county	26.8	26.7	26.7	36.0	49.4	48.6	49.9
	# Eastern region	40.2	45.7	48.1	44.4	44.1	43.6	41.6
	Central region	28.6	23.8	22.9	24.3	22.4	22.6	22.9
	Western region	24.9	21.7	20.6	26.6	29.1	28.7	29.3

The amount of maintenance expenses of national cultural heritage[19] was 24.787 billion yuan, an increase of 1.612 billion yuan, up by 7.0% over that of the previous year; the maintenance expenses of national cultural heritage accounted for 0.17% of China's total financial expenditures, the proportion was basically the same with that of the previous year.

According to the Ministry of Finance of China, of the national financial expenditure in 2014, the amount of expenditure for culture, sports and media[20] was 275.3 billion yuan, up by 9.2% over that of the previous year and accounting for 1.82% of the total financial expenditure, the proportion was basically the same as the previous year.

Figure 10: Aggregate and growth rate of expenditure of national culture , sports and media in 2006-2014

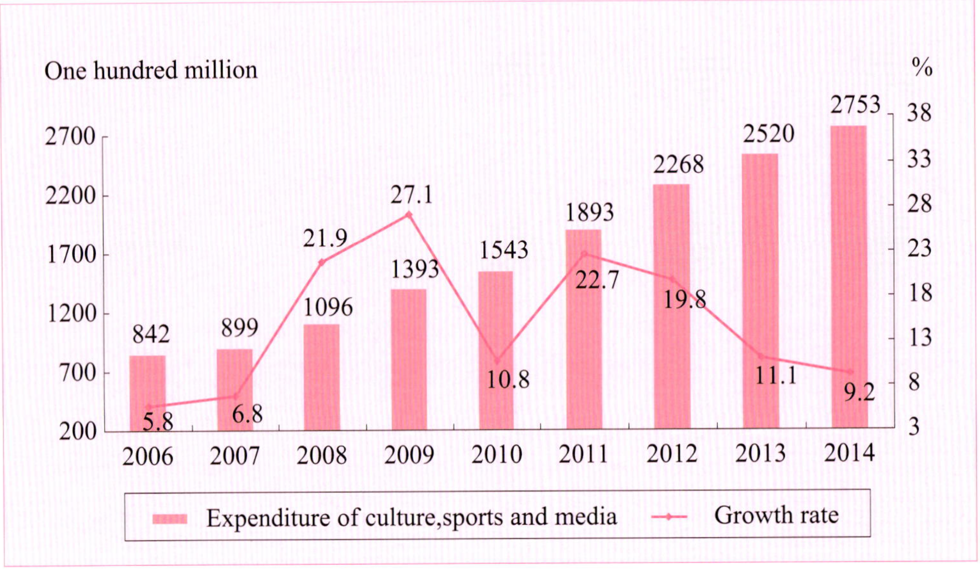

Notes:

[1] All the data of the communiqué are preliminary statistical data. The data of Hongkong SAR, Macao SAR, and Taiwan are not included in this communiqué. Some of data are not compatible with the total of subentries due to rounding off.

[2] Cultural unit refers to cultural institutions that national cultural departments (including cultural system and cultural relic system) of all levels organize or implement industrial management, excluding cultural institutions organized or managed by the departments of all levels of press and publications, radio , film and television, etc. According to the current statistical system, the cultural institutions (such as public libraries, cultural centers, cultural stations, museums, etc.) organized by cultural departments are brought into the statistical range. Regarding cultural institutions with industrial management, the private art performance troupes, cybercafé, and entertainment venues are brought into statistical range, while the mechanism of exchange of works of art, internet culture institution are not in the range.

[3] The employees refer to the people who work and receive working rewards in the institutions that cultural departments at all levels (including cultural systems and cultural relic systems) organize or implement industrial management. The statistical range is ditto with cultural institutions.

[4] Public library refers to all kinds of institutions that are organized by cultural departments at all levels, and is open to public as well as providing popularization and education of science, culture, and other knowledge.

[5] The total collection of books in public libraries refers to the sum of audiovisual literature materials including bound volume, manual, manuscript, micro-reproduction, videotape, audio tape and CD of ancient books, books, periodicals and newspapers in catalogue. It does not include digital books.

[6] The number of library cards issued refers to the number of library cards which are issued by public libraries and used at least once in that very year.

[7] The total flow of person-time of public library refers to the gross person-time of receiving the service of the libraries in that year, including borrowing books, consultation and participating in various readers' activities.

[8] Public and community cultural institutions refer to the places that cultural departments at all levels organize for mass cultural activities, mainly including cultural centers (including comprehensive cultural center and mass art gallery) and cultural stations.

[9] The number of activities means the sum of the organizations of cultural literary and artistic activities, training classes, exhibitions, and public lectures.

[10] Cultural-center-based art groups refer to performance teams composed by the staff of this institution and that provide performances for the mass.

[11] The art performance troupes mean various professional artistic performance organizations which are organized by cultural institutions or to which the cultural institutions implement industrial management (with approval of cultural administration department and commercial performance license), and is engaged in such activities as performing arts.

[12] The operating units of cultural markets refer to the agencies which are approved or filed by administrative departments of cultural markets and have relevant licenses and filing documents, and that engage in cultural management and services. In line with the current statistical systems, the statistical range of operating units of the cultural market only include private art performance troupes, entertainment venues, and business sites of internet access services.

[13] The museum refers to the non-profit and permanent social service institution which collects, preserves, and exhibits the witness of human activity and natural environment with intent of research, education, and appreciation, as well as being open to the public. It includes the units that carry out activities with proper names such as museums, memorial halls, science and technology museums, exhibition halls, etc.

[14] The permanent exhibition refers to the exhibition which is displayed in the pavilion, with fixed location and for an extended time.

[15] The temporary exhibition means the multi-formed exhibition which is set in the institution and designed by the pavilion.

[16] The intangible cultural heritage safeguarding institutions refer to the protection centers of intangible cultural heritage or protection offices of intangible cultural heritage of all levels.

[17] Cultural undertaking expense means aggregate of expenditures that the finance of

all levels in the area invests to the organizer of cultural systems. It generally includes financial appropriation (excluding appropriations of capital construction costs) of cultural institutions such as art performance troupes, public libraries, cultural centers (stations), etc. and financial subsidies of enterprises subordinate to the Ministry of Culture. According to current statistical caliber, cultural operating expense does not include administrative operation expenditures of cultural administration and management departments at all levels.

[18] Eastern region includes Beijing, Tianjin, Liaoning Province, Shanghai, Jiangsu Province, Fujian Province, Shandong Province, and Guangdong Province; Central region includes Hebei Province, Shanxi Province, Jilin Province, Heilongjiang Province, Anhui Province, Jiangxi Province, Henan Province, Hubei Province, Hunan Province and Hainan Province; Western region includes Inner Mongolia (autonomous region), Guangxi Province, Chongqing, Sichuan Province, Guizhou Province, Yunan Province, Tibet (autonomous region), Shannxi Province, Gansu Province, Qinghai Province, Ningxia (autonomous region), and Xinjiang (autonomous region).

[19] The maintenance expenses of national cultural heritage refer to the aggregate of expenditures that the finance departments at all levels in the area invest to the operation of cultural relics. It generally includes financial appropriation (excluding appropriation of capital construction) of operation institutions of cultural relic such as museum, protection and management agencies for cultural relics, etc. and financial subsidies of enterprises subordinate to cultural relic departments.

[20] The data of expenditure of culture, sports and media, which originates from the Ministry of Finance, is the investment of government at all levels in culture, cultural relics, sports, radio, film and television, and press and publications.